Aloneness in Nature

Holly English

Presentation by *BookLeaf Publishing*

Web: www.bookleafpub.com

E-mail: info@bookleafpub.com

ISBN: 9789357214834

First edition 2023

To Everyone

Agreements

Earth, Air, Fire, Water
I stand rooted
I am your daughter

I've howled at the moon
since I was a bae

I've wandered the wood
with fairy at play

I've danced in the flaming
duality of soul

I've harmonized with the river
and its seasonal flow

Inverse of Joy
is to suffer
Beautiful teacher, Gaia Mother

Rise

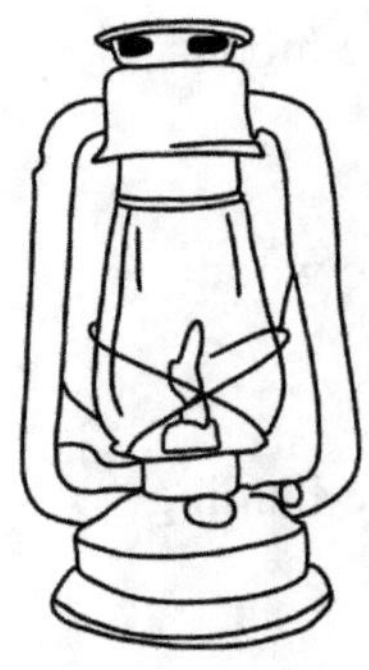

The sun is rising
Let life on Earth coexist
honest vibrations

Set

The sun is setting
The stars are coming outside
The world is asleep

Luna Lessons

I feel the pattern of your lessons, Lady Luna of
old
the eternally divine and precise rhythms you
hold
I cling to your patience as this trail runs cold
Keeping the internal torch lit, resiliently bold

Please guide my feet to the path when I cannot
see
Please pull the tide to release the burdens from
me
As you wax and wane, I cry on bended knee
And one day your fullness set my voice free

There is no going back, no moment is the same
Lady Luna must flow and Father Time takes no
blame
There is wisdom found in their forever game
Within one's soul purpose there is no shame

Owl

The moon is rising
Owl greets the starry sky
A dark world awakes

Changes

Maple Abundance
green, yellow, orange and brown
swirl to the ground

Dear Universe

Dear Universe,

I trust you. I know that everything is as it should be in this moment.

I understand that I cannot escape your turbulent duality, as it is a part of me too.

Mmmmm...Thank you for this time as I find acceptance of this infinite truth that guides my own moral layer.

Just as you provide dense everchanging colors to be in awe of, they reflect within me a tapestry of ancestral emotions.

Changing colors of the weather is the very fabric of my essence.

I too can expand in a moment of pure joy
and contract and fall in moments of weighted sorrow.

I flow in time between the abyss of light and the vastness of dark,
swirling in and out of the astral eddy lines of gripping memories.

Finding meaning in the hydraulics of synchronized indifferences.

Memory

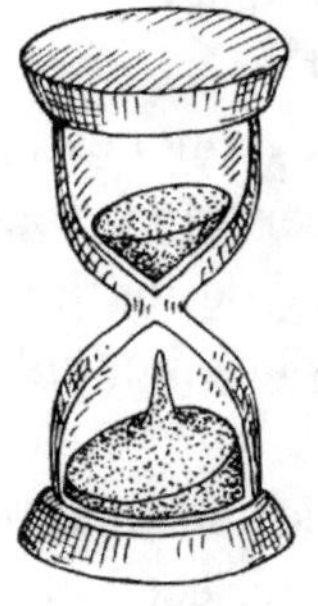

Water Memory
cycling strong emotions
dynamic timelines

Snow

Snow, snow coming down
Swirling, dancing to the ground
quiet peace, no sound

Hibernate

Retreat, it's natural to hibernate
Pushing causes excess at a rapid rate
There is no escape from time and fate
Hibernate to reflect and integrate
Patterned lessons with a refreshed slate

Whispers

Whispers through the trees
Ancestors are guiding us
Forever as one

Solstice

Another solstice
Souls darkness and gracious light
Days sun, starry night

Purpose

Sing with the birds
Alchemy of soul to the song
Spin a web spider mama
Intentions so strong

Such simple integrity
No energy to waste
in gratitude with purpose
Steady without haste

Dance

Flora and Fauna
Together forever dance
Blissful Energy

Sugar

Stretch up to the light
Sunbeams spun into sugar
Sweet, sweet energy

Childhood Love

Reflecting on my childhood love,
lying in the clover.
Sending dandelion wishes above
mulling purpose over.

Flying maple tree helicopters
dancing through a storm
climbing trees like book chapters
watching decay destroy the form

Reflecting on my childhood love
and the wild flowing rivers.
Heavy waves heave and shove,
as the undercurrent quivers.

Emotions envelop like water
perception of the old form
floods have washed out the daughter
worn landscape leaves memories torn

Reflecting on my childhood love,
ever-changing with the stars.
Hard-earned lessons from above
shifting galaxies, beautiful scars.

Pack

Familiar spirits
in your ivy-covered dens
we meet at new moon

History

History in trees
inner growth rings leave time stamps
cycles as circles

Valley

In the shadow of a mountain
under the shade of mighty trees
the light was so high above
with a deafening constant breeze

Surviving in the darkness
chaotic attachments of a constant storm
Rocks roll down to the valley floor
causing growth in distorted form

Seasonal wildfire charges the valley
wreaking havoc, fear and pain
only roots left under soil's cover
Integrated beauty comes with rain

Minimized structure of exposed life
Initiation to blossom alone and within
Let go of rigidity to grow free
Is where joyous truth will begin

Unearthed and raw can feel so right
as the misguided ego stumbles
Vibrant and new from the ashes of youth
humbling lessons in all that crumbles

Glisten

Fog for forty days
The grey foothills of mountains
Sun glistens emeralds

Constant

Golden sun above
AHO strong steady father
Wake with your rhythm